Don't ⌐ ⌐⌐ On The Ants!

Karen Kennedy

Illustrations Credit – Stephen Hayes
Editing – Jeff Zurcher
Technical – Charles H. Foertmeyer III

ISBN – 13: 978-0692605240 (Custom Universal)
ISBN – 10: 069260524X
Don't Step On The Ants

Printed by CreateSpace

Facebook - Moo Moo's Values Book

In Memory

Inspiration

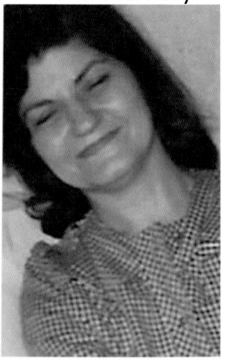

Evie

Tammi

"Thanks for teaching me
not to step on the ants."

Autographs

_____

_____

_____

_____

_____

_____

_____

_____

_____

_____

Dedicated to…Grandchildren
Tony and Faith

Gratitude to...

Illustrations Credit – Stephen Hayes
Editing–Jeff Zurcher

Gratitude—E. Thomas Arington, Prasco
Pharmaceuticals Co., Mason, Ohio

Gratitude—Linda Lea Kennedy—Web
Consultation, Regal Response

Gratitude—Starbucks Coffee, Madeira, Ohio—
Writing Atmosphere

Gratitude—Family and Friends—Loyal
Supporters

Gratitude—C.H. Foertmeyer, Author—
Technical Management

Author's Note

Karen Kennedy is a freelancer from Cincinnati, Ohio. In her children's book, "Don't Step On The Ants," Karen has used her own experience to illustrate the powerful impact of teaching kindness to young children, by starting with the most vulnerable of insects, a tiny ant. The effects, however, are enormous!

My daughter, Tammi wrote, "Thank you for teaching me not to, "step on the ants" and described the importance of this single learning moment as a youngster. In elementary school, I observed her walking home on her tiptoes, avoiding the ants the day after having this discussion!

Kennedy realized the overwhelming strength of these early lessons even more, when years later, her daughter expressed how it had impacted her life. She stated that ongoing "kindness coaching" was instrumental in making important decisions as an independent, young adult.

Karen is a proud grandmother of two children, who are also being shown the impact of caring. "My mother, Evie, started it all", Karen said.

Moo Moo's examples of kindness and compassion are silly, exaggerated and honest. This is a tale with a constructive message that children will love to read again and again!

Preface

We are born with the capacity for empathy and kindness. Teaching kindness toward animals is an important lesson in early development. It is, most often, one of the first lessons in empathy that a child can receive. It demonstrates the importance of the prevention of cruelty to animals as well as illustrates how to respect all living things, including our fellow man. If we raise children who learn and develop kindness and empathy, the "bully" crisis could be stifled significantly. Compassionate children learn not to intimidate.

"Don't Step On The Ants" is a representation of a path we all cross as children and adults every single day where someone or something is vulnerable. Do we choose kindness or empathy or the more adverse choice...become the tormenter?

Moo Moo, the kind dog, addresses this important question as vulnerability crosses her path. She goes to great and excessive lengths to show empathy and kindness to all living creatures, great and small, like the ant...Kindness matters!

Table of Contents

Remember...Don't Step On The Ants!

Please be careful! Please…you just can't!

Please, oh please, <u>don't step on the ants!</u>

Cute and fuzzy and likes to squirm.

Please don't step on the wooly worm!

Peep–peep...there are six!

Please don't step on the six chicks!

Caution...grown-up pollywog!

Please don't step on the cute little frog!

Oink! He's dirty and stinks quite a bit.

Please don't step on the pink piglet!

He moves slowly and is walking in a circle.

Still, please don't step on the hard-shell turtle!

Ride the lift...go up, up, up!

Please, please, please don't step on the pup!

She wears a fur mask in the light of the moon.

Please don't step on the black–striped raccoon!

Demonstrate your holiday cheer.

Please don't step on the festive reindeer!

Wow! Somehow...

Please don't step on the cow!

She's strong and gruff, so handle with care.

Please don't step on the furry, brown bear!

Her ears are big, like flaps on a tent.

Please don't step on the elephant!

Ride high in the sky to see him laugh.

Please don't step on the longneck giraffe!

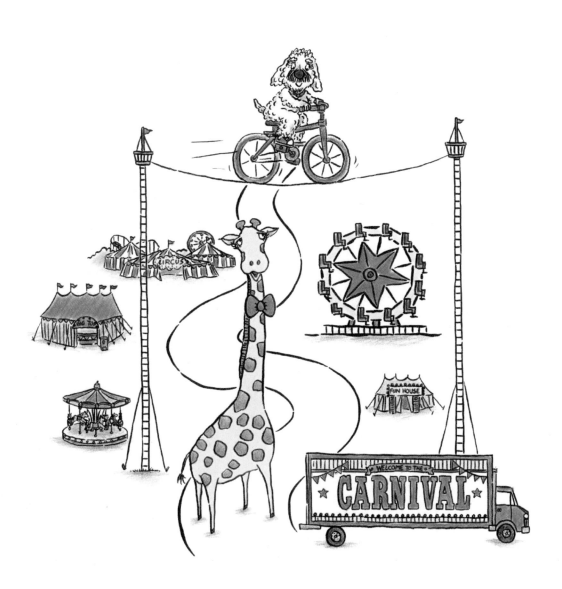

He may be the last...there may be no more.

So, please, don't step on the dinosaur!

Look out for the feelings of sisters and brothers.

Please don't step on the hearts of others!

No matter the creature, great or small.

Please show kindness to one and all.

Kindness does matter...and love makes the difference. So please, let me ask your assistance!

Please Remember...

"Don't Step On The Ants!"

Made in the USA
Monee, IL
22 May 2023

34015456R00029